Battling for Everything

And Planning to Win

By: Greg Phillips

© 2019 by Gregory L. Phillips

For Bulk Ordering and Press Inquiries
Greg Phillips
225-246-5753
glpequippinglackmen@gmail.com

All rights reserved.
No part of this publication may be reproduced, distributed, or transmitted, in any form or by any means, including photocopying, recording, or other electronic or mechanical methods, without prior written permission of the publisher, except in the case of brief quotations, embodied in critical reviews and certain other noncommercial uses permitted by copyright law.

ISBN 978-0-9910648-5-4
Library of Congress Control Number 2020901950

Tonia Askins International LLC
Cultivate Press
3001 Ormond Blvd. Ste. F-7
Destrehan, LA 70047
1-866-553-8746
books@cultivatepress.com

FORWARD

by Milton LaDay

Battling for Everything and Planning to Win is a *call to action*. It is a book to challenge black men to become better by cleaning up the chaos in their personal lives.

I've had the privilege of knowing Greg since 2015. It is an honor that he values my friendship and opinion which means a great deal to me. I am grateful that God would trust me to be a part of his journey. Greg is a man that is very passionate about the things of God. His wisdom and knowledge of God's word amazes me. I encountered many people who have knowledge of God's word, but very few know how to apply and walk in the understanding of it such as Greg.

I'm reminded of Hebrews 4:2 that says, "For we also have had the message preached to us, just as they did; but the message they heard was of no value to them, because those who heard did not combine it with faith."

I have no doubt that the Lord (Jesus) has purposed in Greg's heart to write this book which highlights principles that black men can use to overcome their personal issues and push forward to a better life. This book provides a viable solution to the black man's plight here in the United States of America.

Greg's personal experiences coupled with his wisdom and understanding of God's word has equipped him to speak profoundly on this subject. This book explores God's word by focusing specifically on the battle of David and Goliath. David defeated Goliath by using successful principles that are still available, today, for those who choose to learn and use them.

Battling for Everything and Planning to Win will inspire readers to look within and know that every human being has an innate ability along with God's guidance to make a better life. There is much to glean and learn, how Greg used these principles to overcome obstacles, from this book. This book is practical, valuable, and timely.

I admonish you to read with the intention to learn and then apply the principles to your life as you fight for a better life.

INTRODUCTION

April 17, 2019 the population of North America is 328,617,927 people. In 2006 the population reached 300 million with great fanfare. It took 13 years for the population to grow by another 28 million people. But as I sit in CC's Coffee House in Baton Rouge, Louisiana on my 52nd birthday, I am thinking about the black community as I write the book *Battling for Everything and Planning to Win*.

It has been 154 years since the Emancipation Proclamation. 65 years since the Supreme Court ruled that segregation in public school was unconstitutional. 58 years since the Affirmative Action laws were created. 55 years since the signing of the Civil Rights Acts. And from 2008 to 2016 the United States elected its first black President— Barack Obama.

In 2019, with all of these things that were done to improve the lives of black people here in the United States of America, how much has the black population grown as a race? Are we better off as a race? Or, Are we worse off?

We, the black race, make up approximately 14% of the United States population. That is roughly a little more than 46 million black people. Where do we rank in area of achieving the great American dream? Where do we rank in the area of education? Where do we rank in the area of marriage and divorce? Where do we rank in the area of economics? Where do we rank in the area of employment? Where do we rank in the area of parenting? Where do we rank in the area of the justice system? Where do we rank in the area of ownership, of any kind?

At age 52, I see and hear that we are still fighting many of the same battles that we were fighting when I was a child and before I was born, which indicates, to me, that we are still just *surviving* in a country where we should be *thriving* as a race. Some of the same past solutions are being championed as the cure for the persistent issues that stop us from advancing as a race.

How is it that some of us are able to become more in life than what we started out with in life? How is it that some of us are able to thrive in the United States that many say is a racist nation? How is it that some of us are able to be successful in a country that is said to be a place where only white people can succeed because of "white privilege"?

How is it that black folks like Robert F. Smith, Oprah Winfrey, Jay Z, and Ben Johnson could obtain the status of **Billionaires**? Did these black people receive a "PASS" from white people that gave them permission to be successful here in the US? And if so, who do you talk to and where do you apply for such a thing? And how many black folks are permitted to be successful annually by white folks?

I believe that if we are to be a better people, we must take full responsibility for our destiny and not leave it to others. We have what it takes to be a better people. We have the capability to be a better people. We have the endurance to be a better people.

It is imperative that we fight to be a better people. It is equally imperative that black men wake up and take the lead in making the black race a better race.

For too long, we as black men have abdicated our leadership responsibility to the black woman. The black woman has done what she could in the absence of the black man.

She has been the mother, the father, the provider, the nurturer, the disciplinarian, the spiritual provider, and many other things necessary to keep the home together.

Where has the black man been? And where is the black man now? In my opinion, the black man has lost his way. The chaos in the black community is a direct reflection of the chaos that is going on in the life of the black man. When we, as black men, clean up the *chaos* in our personal lives, we will begin to clean up the *chaos* that is so prevalent in our communities.

Battling for Everything and Planning to Win is a book written specifically for black men. It is a book to inspire black men to find their way out of their personal chaos so that they can reclaim their God given authority they gave away, no matter the reason. This book was born out of my personal experiences through life's journey as I struggled through my process, for years, of cleaning up the chaos in my life and reclaiming my God given authority.

If we, as black men, don't take charge of our lives we can forget about making the black race a better race. Our black women and black children are screaming for us to rise up as men and take our rightful place as leaders to lead them to the promise land of having a better life.

Black men, the spotlight is on us to perform differently and effectively in changing our lives for the better.

Turn the page and let's get started!!!

CHAPTER 1

BATTLING FOR EVERYTHING HAS ROOTS IN LEARNING HOW TO FIGHT FROM A YOUNG AGE.

"One of the servants answered. 'I have seen a son of Jesse of Bethlehem who knows how to play the lyre. He is a *brave* man and a *warrior*. He speaks well and is a fine-looking man. And the Lord is with him.'" (*NIV,* 1Sa 16:18)

"DeDe! Momma had a white baby!" Ramona yelled to my other sister.

My mother went to the hospital to give birth but was sent home because the doctors deemed that she was not ready. However, when my mother returned home, she soon gave birth to me in my grandmother's bed.

The story about my birth was foreshadowing my future filled with many twists and turns.

I spent several years living with my grandmother where everything was provided to me. I had no worries, my bath water was always prepped, and I was given three meals a day.

Then around the age of 5, I moved to my mom's house. In contrast to my grandmother's home, I had to learn how to fend for myself. My mom had to support 5 kids ranging in age 5 to 13. Everyone in the house had to learn to pull their own weight and I learned what it was like to become independent and not dependent.

Independence and fearlessness did not come easily. Around age 7 I developed a serious stuttering problem and I was bullied every day by two of my classmates.

The bullying was stopped when my brother challenged me to stand up against my classmates, which I did. I found it hard to express myself because I was unable to get words out of my mouth. The problem was so frustrating, that I would literally have to beat on things and people to help formulate my words. If you did not know me, you would have thought that I was hitting you to be a bully.

I don't remember being self-conscience about my stuttering to the point where I did not want to talk. If anything, I was willing to do anything, including hurting others in order to get my words out. I figured I had the right to talk like everybody else did; therefore, I was determined to talk at any cost. I would speak no matter how long it took me to get my words out of my mouth.

Eventually, with the help of the school's Speech Pathologist, I overcame stuttering while I was still in elementary school. As a matter of fact, by the time I entered fifth grade I no longer had a stuttering problem. I was speaking normally just like all the other children.

In 1977, my childhood would change forever at age ten. My oldest sister, Denise, gave birth to Daymond, my oldest nephew. However, just after a few months of motherhood, my sister decided that she no longer wanted to be a mother, so she handed Daymond over to my mother and walked out on her responsibility.

My mother being, kind, loving, and generous received her first grandson and raised him as her son. When my mother took up the responsibility of raising Daymond, that meant the entire household took on the responsibility. Momma still had to work long hours to make ends meet and support her growing family.

In the beginning of our adjustment period, there were four of us taking turns caring for Daymond. Then it went from four to me, by then my three older siblings had moved out of the house and started their own lives.

Nevertheless, by the time I started junior high school, I had experienced many things that were forcing me to grow up rapidly and raising a child while being a child was a major battle for a 10-year-old. This battle would last for eight years; right up to the time I left my mother's house at age 18.

To this day, Daymond calls his grandmother 'Momma' and for many years he would refer to his birthmother by her first name. However, over the years, Daymond learned to forgive his mother and before the death of both my sister and my mother they were able to hear Daymond call his mother, 'Mommy!!'

In my formative years, the primary tool that probably taught me the most about fighting, was from neighborhood sports. As children, we played basketball, football, and baseball. Even the occasional game of dominos was considered a competitive sport in my neighborhood.

Around the age of 6, I remember, Buddy, Darrell, and me often ended up on the same team. Our lessons came from Freddie Byrd... he was our leader, guide, and director. For 5 years, Freddie played a strong and memorable role in our young lives. His lessons served us well then and continues to serve us in our adult lives.

More than a few times, we would find ourselves playing against older and bigger guys; however, we won many games that we had no business winning. *Why?* We learned from Freddie how to develop methods and strategies that would somehow level the playing field.

Losing a few times and being bullied around also helped convince us that losing was not a good thing to master.

We recognized that losing meant we were at the bottom and being at the bottom did not feel good. Therefore, we had to learn how to win and win more than one time so there was no doubt in the minds of our opponents that we could play with them and beat them. Beating them is what we did on a regular basis, whether it was in football, basketball, baseball, or dominos, it made no difference to us.

We had to be quick learners and we had to learn as we played. Our mistakes were our best teachers.

Now, at the time of playing the neighborhood sports, I did not know how important the lessons from sports were to my life. To be honest, I just wanted to be part of a winning team. I wanted to be picked somewhere at the top because I thought the good players were all at the top.

Little did I know that it would be the bottom half that proved to be the cream of the crop. It would be the less chosen ones who would be the envy of the neighborhood or the ones who would set a standard that everyone was trying to surpass. Who would have thought it—not Buddy, Darrell or Greg!

CHAPTER 2

BATTLING FOR EVERYTHING REQUIRES BEING AT PEACE WITH BEING UNCOMFORTABLE.

"[28]When Eliab, David's oldest brother, heard him speaking with the men, he burned with anger at him and asked, 'Why have you come down here? And with whom did you leave those few sheep in the wilderness? I know how conceited you are and how wicked your heart is; you came down only to watch the battle.' [29] 'Now what have I done?' said David. 'Can't I even speak?' [30]He then turned away to someone else and brought up the same matter, and the men answered him as before. What David said was overheard and reported to Saul, and Saul sent for him." (1 Sa 17:28-30)

In my 52 years of living I have come to whole heartily agree with the song "Joy and Pain", sang by the R&B group Maze and Frankie Beverly.

Over and over you can be sure...

There will be sorrow, but you will endure...

Where there's a flower there's the sun and the rain...

Oh, and it's wonderful they're both one in the same

Before obtaining the joy of attaining, there will be many days and nights filled with much pain and uncertainty.

Dr. Kelso said, "Life is scary. Get used to it. There are no magical fixes; it's all up to you. So, get up off your keister and start doing the work. Nothing in this world that's worth having comes easy."

We are living in a time where many desire success, but they want it without experiencing the agony of defeat. If you never experience defeat, you are playing it safe. Playing it safe eliminates pain, strife, failure, disappointment, and discomfort from one's life; however, playing it safe in life leads to a false sense of security and living a mediocre life.

The people that play it safe in life are the people that have regrets at the end of their lives. The common phrase used among people that play it safe in life is "I wish I had done..." Long ago I decided that at the end of my life I would have no regrets because I would do everything that my heart desired.

When I decided to battle for my heart's desires, I decided to be *comfortable* with being *uncomfortable*. In other words, I learned to be at peace with experiencing pain, strife, misunderstandings, setbacks, failure, delays, sleepless night, homelessness, divorce, being broke, rejections, and any other discomfort I experienced while pursuing worthy goals.

It seemed as though the more I got burned by life, for wanting to improve my life, the more I pushed to move forward to obtain my life changing goals.

In May of 1995, I graduated from Abilene Christian University with a Bachelor Degree in Theology/Missiology with an overall 3.3 GPA. This was a great accomplishment, but it took me ten years to do so. Before I graduated from College, I experienced a lot of heartaches along the way.

I flunked out of LSU, not once but twice. I took the ACT three times and each time I took it my score went down. I had to take remedial classes before I could start taking classes towards my degree. I stepped away from school for three years to discover the direction I wanted my life to go in.

Part of that direction was getting married and starting a family that I had to support. Not everyone believed in me or supported my decision to finish school. I faced many financial adversities while trying attend classes and support a family at the same time. I had to sacrifice many family functions and personal enjoyment to pursue my degree. Once I received my degree, all of my hardships could not compare to the joy I felt when I walked across the stage to receive my diploma.

In August of 1995, after I graduated from ACU, my family and I moved to San Jose, Costa Rica. One year later, I received a certificate in Spanish from El Instituto de Lengua de Espanol.

My family and I attended this school for one year to learn the Spanish language because we were preparing ourselves to be missionaries in Venezuela. This was anything but easy. At the time, my son, Caleb was 3 and Angel, my daughter was 1. There were many days that I thought I had lost my mind for dragging my family to an unfamiliar country where in the beginning we could not communicate because we did not speak Spanish.

Costa Rica was a humbling experience. I must admit that I was afraid, but I could not make my fear known to my wife, Andrea or to our children. After all, we were in Costa Rica because of my belief that God had led us there. It was too late for me to change my mind and return home, so I did what I had being doing my entire life. I move forward.

I challenged myself to learn the language quickly and effectively, so I hired a tutor to coach me with extra lessons 3 days a week.

Considering we lived a mile and a half from the school, in a gated community, where everyone spoke only Spanish, I was forced to practice what I was learning. There were a few people in that community who spoke English, but they refused because they knew we were in their country to learn Spanish.

To be honest, we made complete fools of ourselves learning Spanish. But doing those foolish things paid off, after eleven months of living in Costa Rica we were able to speak, write, and read fluent Spanish. In July of 1996, we moved to Venezuela from Costa Rica to begin our work as missionaries.

In April of 1998, after living in Venezuela for nearly 2 years, the dream of being a missionary came crashing down around me like a ton of bricks. The missionary team I was a part of was dysfunctional. We all had the same goal but different agendas. I returned home with my family in tow. I was a missionary with no direction of what I was going to do for work. I had a wife and two children to support.

After returning home, my family and I would experience several major traumas that would change the trajectory of my life.

In May of 1998 Andrea's parents lost their house and everything they owned in a house fire. In August of 1998, Andrea lost a sister, 2 nephews, and a niece in a car accident in one day.

In that same accident, her mother, and two nieces were injured for life.

Twenty-one years have passed since the accident and Andrea's mother has never driven again, a niece is paralyzed, and the other niece was left without a mother or brother.

In September of 1998, Andrea and I would separate for a period of time than reunite; however, in 2001 Andrea would divorce me, leaving us to go our separate ways after 12 years of marriage.

Divorce would change the direction of my life for many years. After losing my wife and my ministry, I realized that I had lost my identity. I could not recognize who I was as a man and who I was professionally.

I was no longer a husband or a minister. My Identity, my passion, my convictions were all gone. As a matter of fact, my pain, anger, and confusion drove me to become somewhat of a womanizer while searching for a career I could be passionate about.

Finally, in 2018, after twenty years of wondering and fighting to find purpose for my life, I finally found my passion. After many years of hardships, pain, anger, sadness, and confusion, God had mercy on me and brought me back to my first passion— The Ministry!!! The writing of this book is part of my ministry rebirth.

CHAPTER 3

BATTLING FOR EVERYTHING GOES WELL BEYOND CRYING AND COMPLAINING ABOUT YOUR PERSISTENT SITUATION.

"Now the Israelites had been saying, 'Do you see how this man keeps coming out? He comes out to defy Israel.'" (1 Sa 17:25b)

Anthony J. D'Angelo said, *"If you have time to whine and complain about something then you have time to do something about it."*

I have personally found that if you don't like something about your life you need to do something positive to change it. I have seen and been around many people who only cry and complain about their unpleasant situation. It is as though they are under the belief that crying and complaining are great tools to use to change unpleasant situations in life.

News flash... Life is unfair! As a matter of fact, life is so unfair that while you are crying and complaining about one unpleasant problem, life will inevitably hand you another one to deal with. The sun will rise from the east and set in the west every day. Life goes on no matter what.

From 1998 to 2005, a total of seven years, life had dealt me one problem after another. In this seven year period, I lost my job, I lost my marriage, I went from job to job, I had to deal with legal issues, I was very close to being homeless, I had to fight to be a father to my children, I had my youngest son with another woman while my ex-wife and I were going through our divorce, many friends turned their backs to me and stopped talking to me, and to escape my pain I created pain by becoming a womanizer. Nevertheless, with all of my problems, I had learned not to complain about them to others because it was wasted energy to do so.

It is a fact that I did not like my situation in life, but I refused to waste time crying about it and feeling sorry for myself. Every day I got up and went to work no matter what type of work it was for me to do. I put all of my energy and focus on trying to improve my life by redefining my life.

In that fateful year, 1998 I remember silently pleading with God and life to slow down so I could at least take a breath, but it never did. Every day the sun kept rising and setting as scheduled. No matter how much I despised, complained, and cried about my hell on earth, the problems persistently came at me.

Depression wrapped its arms around me and took ahold of me for years... It went to bed with me... It woke up with me... It went to work with me... It ate and drank with me... It had fun with me... Depression was with me 24 hours a day, 7 days a week, never leaving my side for three and half years.

In August of 2005, Hurricane Katrina would bring devastation, destruction, death, and dislocation to many that lived in the New Orleans area. My children and I were some of these people. We were not part of the many folks that needed to be rescued. Katrina made landfall on an early Monday morning, we left the New Orleans area the day before.

We left for my hometown in Alexandria, Louisiana. It took us 4 hours to get from New Orleans to Alexandria, normally a 3-hour drive. We drove all back roads since I-10 had turned into a parking lot, trapping many trying to flee the wrath of Katrina.

Just before hurricane Katrina made landfall, I had become a real estate agent and I started learning about business. I was reading one and two books a week about becoming successful in business.

I also started to put a Spanish curriculum together so that I could start a business teaching people the Spanish language. So, when my children and I were forced to evacuate to Alexandria, I was somewhat armed with the ability to make a living as a real estate agent and a Spanish teacher... or so I thought.

Once we started living and settling down in Alexandria, I started promoting my Spanish business. I would do two spots on the local morning television show called *Jambalaya*. I had a few commercials playing on the local radio station. Although I was far from being financially stable to support my kids and myself, I never succumbed to the pressure of viewing myself as a victim like so many who were experiencing the after-effects of Hurricane Katrina.

A reporter for the local newspaper, *The Town Talk* was looking to interview evacuees from New Orleans. After hearing some of my story, I was informed I was not the type of *victim* they were looking for and were never interested in interviewing me.

Even though I was willing to fight to build my business in Alexandria, it never happened like I had in mind. I gave it my all, but my all was not good enough. So nearly 2 years of living in Alexandria, I moved to Houston, Texas with another mark against me in the failure and disappointment column.

In the summer of 2007, I boarded a Greyhound bus bound for Houston with no job lined up to support myself. I was excited to be closer to my youngest son and to get a fresh start.

Although I had new surroundings my problems were very persistent. However, within one month of living in Houston, I did secure a sales job. I started selling health and life insurance using public transportation to get me from one appointment to the next.

My oldest son, Caleb soon moved to Houston to be with me and experience the good times as well as the bad times. Caleb was in the 10th grade. I was making enough money to take care of our basic needs, but not enough to buy furniture for the apartment I was able to secure for us.

All we had were air mattresses to sleep on and two folding chairs to sit on while we watched TV on my son's PSP. We spent many hours reading books at Barnes & Nobles and going to the Dollar Theatre every weekend.

These were some tough days, but my son and I never complained about our miserable situation. One day, I remember telling my son, "Look, this is not a pleasant situation. If all of this is too unbearable for you, all you have to do is say so. You can go back to New Orleans with your momma."

Caleb looked me in the eyes and said, "Daddy, I have come this far with you, I don't plan to leave you now." To be honest, I was pleasantly surprised by his response and greatly encouraged by his words. I needed to hear those words from my son because it gave me hope that my striving to improve our lives had purpose and meaning for the both of us.

Eventually, after Caleb's 10th grade year, he chose to move back to New Orleans to finish his last two years of high school at the same school his mother graduated from back in 1983.

When he left, I missed him greatly, but I was encouraged that Caleb was on the right path to do great things in his life. Twelve years later, Caleb has become the man I had envisioned him to be. He has a family of his own, he is a daddy to his son, and a faithful husband to his wife.

He has a pilot's license to be a tugboat captain and he also works with doctors and their staff to be more effective in patience care via a computer program. He flies all over the US doing this job. I am very proud of the man he has become.

I have to say, Caleb had to endure the personal hardships we faced in Houston before he could achieve getting the life that he wanted for himself.

After Caleb returned to New Orleans my life continued to be plagued with problems in Houston. By this time, I began working for Macy's selling women's shoes. I was able to buy myself a vehicle and move to Katy Texas. I enjoyed nine months with no major problems in my life.

Nevertheless, this would soon change. Selling women's shoes at Macy's slowed down tremendously. I stayed longer than I should have, especially when my pay was based on commission, because I was told that the downward cycle, we were in was a normal cycle; however, the downward cycle lasted longer than expected.

Therefore, in April of 2009, in the course of one week —because of lack of car payments--my car was repossessed, I lost my job because I had no transportation to get there, and I lost my apartment because I could not pay my rent, leaving me homeless.

There was no regular public transportation between Katie and Houston. While living in Katie when things were going well, I was attending a church called Faith Manager. Once I became homeless, it was this church that the Bishop allowed me to sleep in his office, I will be forever grateful for the kindness he showed me. I lived liked this for one month until I secured a place to live.

After being homeless for one month, I was able to find a job and a place to live in Katy, Texas. I started selling Kirby vacuum cleaners and renting a bedroom in the home of a friend of the Bishop's wife. In one month, I sold 15 vacuum cleaners, earning enough money to pay my bills and to buy me a bus ticket for San Diego, California where my brother had been living for more than 20 years.

June of 2009, I found myself on a Greyhound bus, only this time, I was leaving Houston and heading to San Diego to help my brother run a Security company. Thirty-six hours after leaving Houston I arrived in San Diego on a Saturday morning with my brother waiting for me. The following Monday I started working as a security officer.

It was true he got me in the door of the security job, but it was my work ethic that kept me in the job for the two full years I lived in San Diego. My work ethic also allowed me to advance into leadership positions and to work as the point person to begin a new security site for the company and stabilize an ailing security site. My brother and I worked as though we were the owners of the business.

We worked in San Diego, El Cojon, Ervine, LA, and Valejo. There were times we would have to work 72-hours without sleep to rectify problems that were created by security guards that lacked our same work ethic.

I remember we had a contract with a construction company working on a major building project at the University of Cal in Ervine California.

We had 72-hours to rectify theft issues that resulted from our security guards inability to perform their jobs. Approximately $10,000 dollars of appliances were stolen from the property under the watch of our security guards. Not one guard had an explanation on how this happened. Not one guard saw $10,000 worth of appliance leave the premises.

Needless to say, my brother fired every security guard that was on site except Mr. T. He was about to quit because he had not received any pay after completing two-weeks of work.

Now, Mr. T was not depending upon this money to live because he had retired from General Motors after a 30-year career. He was only working security to keep himself active. Nevertheless, he deserved his money for the service he had rendered to the company. Because this security site was managed by corrupt and incompetent managers, Mr. T's time sheet was never submitted to the company's business department.

My brother and I recognized that Mr. T was a man of integrity and someone we needed on the team to turn that site around so we would not lose the contract. We were able to convince Mr. T that things would get better and my brother was able to get him his check immediately. He was part of the plan to make things better.

After the initial 72-hours, my brother was able to hire some quality people that possessed the desired work ethic we needed.

The people that made the difference were: Mr. T our lead person for day shift, Ron (guard for day shift), Torri (lead person for weekend), Ray Washington, the general manager, and myself the supervisor for the site.

We had full authority to make the necessary changes without being undermined. The guard shed at the main site was used for two purposes. First it was used for the posting of the supervisor and lead person.

Second, it was used as a place to sleep, mainly for me as the supervisor. I slept at the site every day except weekends. It was also used for Torrie to sleep on the weekends. Torrie lived about 3 or 4 hours away from the site; therefore, she worked weekends only. I supervised that site for close to a year and Torrie never called in to say that she was not coming to work. Outside of Mr. T, Torrie was the best worker—hands down.

After 8 months of working this site, it became stabilized, allowing me to put my attention on other things like my personal life. By this time, I had been a single man for about nine years.

March 2010, I connected with Angela Coleman, one of my high school classmates via Facebook two weeks after the death of her father. In

April 2010, I decided to take a chance and travel to Louisiana to meet with Angela in person. We spent a few days together to see if there was chemistry between us. I was happy I took the chance because there was a spark between us.

After returning to California, we continued to talk and when I flew back to Louisiana to attend my oldest son's graduation, I took Angela with me.

In June and July, I made more trips to Louisiana to spend time with Angela. By the time August rolled around, enough time had passed that Angela knew enough about my character and what type of man I was. She did not hesitate to make a trip to California to visit me.

I cannot say the same for Angela's siblings. When she came out to visit, she had to give my contact information or my brother's contact information to anyone in her family.

We had a great time together. Angela got to see some of the security sites I managed. We also spent time in Hollywood and at the beautiful beach at Oceanside. It was after her visit to California that I started making plans to move back to Baton Rouge.

In January 2011, I moved back to Baton Rouge and on June 20, 2015 Angela Coleman became my wife. In seventeen years, I had experienced a lot of lows in my life that caused anger, sadness, broken heartedness, depression, frustration, and many other ill emotions that accompany dealing with death, unemployment, divorce, and homelessness.

In spite of all the hard times and ill feelings, I was able to work through these heart wrenching traumas' and develop strategies to help me improve my life. My marriage to Angela and my continuation of pursuing life changing goals were proof that I had learned that battling for everything went well beyond crying and complaining about persistent issues.

CHAPTER 4

BATTLING FOR EVERYTHING REQUIRES USING THE UNSEEN WORLD TO CHANGE THE SEEN WORLD.

"David said to the Philistine, 'You come against me with sword and spear and javelin, but I come against you in the name of the Lord Almighty, the God of armies of Israel, whom you have defied. This day the Lord will deliver you into my hands, and I'll strike you down and cut off your head. All those gathered here will know that it is not by sword or spear that the Lord saves; for the battle is the Lord's and he will give all of you into our hands.'" (1 Sa 17:45-47)

"Each of us is here to discover our true Self, that essentially we are spiritual beings who have taken manifestation in physical form, that we're not human beings that have occasional spiritual experiences, that we're spiritual beings that have human experiences." - Deepak Chopra

In 1995, I graduated from Abilene Christian University with a degree in Theology/Missiology. ACU was a good place for me to get a lot of great knowledge about The God of heaven and earth, but to learn how to tap into the unseen world, I had to have more than head knowledge.

From 1998 to 2018, twenty years, I lived in a wilderness that became my teacher, allowing me to learn about spirituality. My classroom was one that consisted of lots of darkness, mixed with some light, a classroom mixed with many days and nights of pain and some joy.

It was class where the teacher created lessons that were designed for confusion and frustration, with very little clarity. Profanity was the preferred language to help express thoughts among the people I found myself associated with in the wilderness. Because the classroom experiences were so painful, I found myself looking for anything to help escape from the pain keeping me lost in the wilderness.

I found that my ACU experiences could not assist me in my new surroundings. The teachings had become obsolete, leaving me helpless. I was miserable and very angry towards God because he had turned his back on me, leaving me to defend myself with useless tools.

In 2005, after seven years of becoming part of my wilderness. I was in the wilderness because I could not defeat or escape it. I accepted the pain, the anger, the profanity, and the womanizing as my own. In my wilderness, the abovementioned things were defining my life.

Part of me became comfortable living and identifying with the wilderness; however, my *spirit which is from God* would never accept living and identifying with the living conditions of the wilderness— NEVER!!

My spiritual side would put up a strong silent fight to be rescued to gain control of a hellish person that was living in a hellish place because of pain. At night, on occasion, while my conscious mind was distracted with rest, my *spirit* would use my subconscious mind to communicate with its Maker in the unseen world.

There were times I would awake and find myself praying to God who I had dismissed from my life. My spirit was looking for anything it could use to save me from becoming completely dark.

Although I did not consciously plan to look for spiritual reading material to connect me to the spiritual or unseen world, it would happen through my reading of successful businesses and successful people. Because I was striving to improve my life, I began to read about the habits of successful people.. I wanted to be more... I wanted to do more... I wanted to have more. Therefore, I became a self-learner and a life learner to achieve the things I set my heart on.

After studying the habits of successful people, the one thing that all of them had in common was their ability to change their lives by changing themselves from the inside. It was about them changing themselves from the inside out.

They all possessed the ability to use the unseen world to change the seen world. I began to notice the businesses these people were building were really the tools needed to change them from the inside out. Their successful businesses were the result of them successfully changing themselves personally by tapping into the spiritual world.

So, I concluded that if I wanted to be more, if I wanted to do more, and if I wanted to have more then I needed to use the same template that successful people used to become successful in the unseen world.

When my children and I moved to Alexandria during the Katrina days, I was ready to put into action what I had been learning from my readings. In Alexandria, I started a business called Passion for Life, LLC, a Spanish business, among other things, to help people learn the Spanish language and to help them change themselves from the inside out. I then learned that this was not an overnight process and it would take time. My business in Alexandria failed; however, I continued to pursue the concept of using the unseen world to change the seen world while I worked my way through the wilderness that I was living in.

While living in Houston and working as an insurance agent tapping into the spiritual realm was brought to another level when I met Pastor Michael Neal. He was looking to buy health insurance for he and his daughter Olivia. That Wednesday night, I met with Michael Neal will be etched in my mind forever... not because I was unable to close an insurance deal, but because this man was able to tell me personal things about my life that I did not share with him.

In my mind, the only way he could have gotten this information was for him to talk with someone who knew me personally. So, during the course of our conversation I stopped and asked, "Who have you talked to about me?" He chuckled, "Greg, we just met. Who would I call?"

I was astounded and shook my head in disbelief, "I don't understand, how you know so much about me?" He tapped the side of his head, "God is giving me the information as we're sitting here talking."

To say the least, I was at a loss for words and could not respond. I knew deep down he was telling me the truth whether I was ready to hear it or not. It was clear to me that this was no ordinary encounter. This meeting with Pastor Michael convinced me that spiritual beings make their presence known in the physical world on a regular basis with or without our acknowledgement of the presence. This incident would not be the last encounter I would have with the spiritual realm.

After moving back to Baton Rouge from San Diego, I continued to work on being more, doing more, and having more by applying the theory of changing my life via spiritual concepts that I had learned from successful people.

Even though I was using spiritual concepts to improve my life, I was still not interested in repairing my relationship with God. When I returned to Baton Rouge, I worked as a Spanish teacher at a private school called False River Academy for four years.

In 2015, I left the teaching profession and started a vehicular transportation business because it was a better way of being more, doing more, and having more. Through working my own business, I envisioned myself becoming a better me from the inside out. However, this business would fail as well in June of 2018, but for a different reason.

My next two encounters with the spiritual realm would set the stage for my departure of the wilderness that I had been living in since 1998, the year my problems changed my life. I met Milton Laday around the same time I started my transportation business. Milton is a general contractor working for himself for over twenty years. At times Milton would have business meetings at the same CC's Coffee House I frequent, with some of his partners or employees.

Needless to say, I would be eavesdropping on the meetings, simply because I was studying successful people. It took a while, but I eventually decided to strike up a conversation with Milton about his business.

Right away, I could tell Milton would be an excellent resource while I tried to build my small business. I had no idea that Milton's connections went far beyond the earthly realm. Milton is more than a business owner. He is connected to the spiritual realm in ways that will blow your mind and he is very humble with his gift.

I found out about this gift one day in January of 2018. On this day, Milton was not supposed to be at the coffee shop, but he showed up in the afternoon and he found me drinking coffee and reviewing some notes.

The part of our conversation that was out of the ordinary was the part where Milton invited me to his church. My standard response to an invite to church was a stern 'NO' with an explanation of how much I detested church people. I remembered that I stood up from where we were sitting and then Milton said to me, "Wow, I don't know who you are, but God is telling me as you are standing that you are a special man."

I stopped in my tracks and I sat down because Milton's message from God reminded me of the message God gave to Michael Neal about me ten years ago. This encounter did not change my attitude towards God and church, but it did cause me to ponder about the meaning behind the encounter.

Life as it was, would continue for me… meaning I was still working crazy hours fighting to grow my young business. Between the months of January and June, I noticed that I was in a transition. I thought that the transition was business related so I began to search and I found an 18-wheeler with a 7 car hauler that would generate more income for my business.

Soon, I would learn how much I had misinterpreted the transition. In June, the meaning would become clear to me by another encounter with the spiritual realm.

The encounter came Friday, June 1st, 2018, while I was sleeping at a rest area in Van, Texas off interstate 20. On Thursday May 31, 2018, I started traveling to Mesquite, Texas to deliver 3 vehicles that I was transporting on my car hauler.

I stopped at the rest area in Van, Texas around 9:00 that Thursday night and was planning to resume my travels at 6:00 the following morning. This was my regular routine. However, the life changing encounter happened in the early part of Friday morning. What makes this encounter different from the other encounters is that no other human being would deliver the heavenly message. I would get this message directly from God.

The process started around 2:30 in the morning and lasted for about 45 minutes. I was awakened with a heavy feeling of depression along with thoughts of my ex-wife, Andrea. This early morning episode put me in a self-reflective mode. I was seriously trying to find the reason in mind as to why I was depressed and why I was thinking about Andrea. At this time, Andrea and I had been divorced for seventeen years and I had worked my way through my depression many years prior to this incident.

Then, why was I pondering and reflecting on this matter? God entered into my thinking process and revealed to me *why* I was depressed and thinking about my ex-wife. The feeling of depression was really God's tool to get my attention. God explained to me that my anger and distrust was directed towards Him and Him alone. Once I recognized and accepted that, I could not move forward in my life nor could I fulfill the assignment He had for me to do.

> I HAD STOPPED TRUSTING GOD WHEN
> ANDREA DIVORCED ME.

Although I had stop trusting Him, He was faithful to me and never stopped trusting me. Needless to say, I listened, and at a rest stop in the middle of nowhere, I cried like a baby and asked for forgiveness because I had turned my back on God for twenty years.

After the encounter, God removed the pain and anger from my heart and gave me his peace.

As I was traveling back home later that day, I made phone calls to my wife and 3 friends to share the encounter I had with God—in tears as I was explaining. From that day, I have not been the same man.

For many years while I was living in sin and darkness, God used secular books with spiritual concepts to teach me about the unseen spiritual world.

CHAPTER 5

BATTLING FOR EVERYTHING REQUIRES YOU DECIDE TO BE A DIFFERENCE MAKER IN YOUR WORLD.

"David asked the men standing near him, 'What will be done for the man who kills this Philistine and removes this disgrace from Israel? Who is this uncircumcised Philistine that he should defy the armies of the living God?'" (1 Sa 17:26)

"You cannot get through a single day without having an impact on the world around you. What you do makes a difference and you have to decide what kind of difference you want to make." - Jane Goodall

Before we talk about deciding to make a difference in your world, I need to inform you about what that all entails. Making a difference in your world is not easy.

The thing that you want to change will *not change* just because you want it to. When you fight for change, you invite trouble into your life. And trouble will come from every side, including from you. You will constantly doubt yourself because the issue(s) you want to change will get worse before it gets better.

People will think that you are crazy for wanting to make a difference. You will have critics on every side including from people you love. You will be forever misunderstood, simply for the fact that you are doing something about a persistent problem that everyone loves to complain about.

> YOU WILL LEARN THAT PEOPLE THINK WORDS ARE THE SAME AS ACTION SO THEY WILL TALK, TALK, AND TALK ABOUT A PROBLEM, BUT WILL NOT HAVE A PLAN OF ACTION TO DEAL WITH THE PROBLEM.

Now that I got that out of the way... let me ask you a series of questions. As you read these questions take time to think through each one and answer honestly.

In the world where you live, what do you like or do not like about it?

What are some things that everyone considers to be a problem?

Do you consider the perceived problem to be a problem?

Why do you consider the problem to be a real problem?

How important is it for you to be recognized by other people?

Are you easily offended?

Do you have a need to be liked by others?

What are your personal feelings about failure?

Have you ever failed at anything? If yes, how did it make you feel?

What did you do after the failure?

How do you feel about being rejected?

Are you willing to fight on when others have stop fighting because the battle seems to be a lost cause?

How you answer the above questions will determine if you will be successful in making a difference in your world.

In 1975, I was eight years of age when I began to wonder about my biological father. I wanted to know who he was. At this time, I noticed that my siblings and I were calling our grandfather "Daddy", which made me ask myself if he was my biological father.

I concluded that he could not be because all of my family (mother, aunts, and cousins) referred to my grandfather as "Daddy." So, who was my father? This question would drive me and fuel my quest to be a different kind of father.

At an early age, I decided that my children would not have to ask the question of who their father was because I would be in their lives, at all costs. At age 10, my conviction of being a different kind of father was driven deeper within my spirit with the birth of my oldest nephew, Daymond.

I was there when my oldest sister walked out the life of her son because she wanted to live her life without being a mother. From the beginning, Daymond's father was never in the picture.

At the tender age of 10 until the age of 18, God would use my miserable situation of being a father figure for a nephew and later my younger sister Alice as my training ground. My misery trained me well to be a different kind of father.

In 1992, my oldest son Caleb was born. In 1994, my daughter Angel was born. In 2001, my youngest son London was born. The lessons I learned about fatherhood from age 10 to 18 made a huge difference as to how I would be a father to my three children.

You see during my training days I realized that having sex had consequences and the end result of sex was a baby.

> ONCE THE BABY CAME INTO THIS WORLD IT WAS TOO LATE TO DECIDE THAT YOU NEED TO LIVE YOUR LIFE.

The child that was born becomes the focal point. The child's life became your life. Your life was subordinate to the child's life. Life was all about the child. Because my sister went on with her life, that meant somebody else life had to stop to focus on the baby's life.

That somebody was me and the efforts of my other siblings. I just had the longest stint of child caring than the others.

Everything that I did as a child for fun had come to a screeching halt. I recall that when I was playing with friends my attention was always divided between having fun and being a babysitter at the same time.

I also knew which one was most important because whenever the babies cried for attention, I stopped playing in order to give my full attention to the baby. There were many days during this time that I was envious of the freedom my neighborhood friends had. It was so unfair being forced to care for children that I had not produced.

Not to mention the fact that I was still a child myself. I had to learn how to process feelings that I had never felt before. I resented the times my sister would just show up and wanted to become "momma" for a few hours and then leave for days until she needed another "momma" fix.

Because I had a major role in taking care of my nephew and baby sister, I did not have time to deal with adolescent issues like other kids my age. During this time my mother was working long hours at two jobs. She would work like this for many years. Therefore, someone had to pick up the slack at home. After my siblings moved on with their lives, I was the one to pick-up the slack. In just seven short years, I had come a long way since the days of living with my grandmothers in regard to fending for myself.

At age nine, I learned how to cook for myself because my three older sisters would not do it for me. So instead of asking and always hearing "No," I decided to learn how to cook my own food.

My favorite food to cook was a "whole cake" (this is one big pan cake made from flour and water) with eggs and some type of meat to go with it. From the age of nine, I was never dependent on anyone to cook me a meal.

As a matter of fact, on some Wednesdays, my mother would allow Buddy and me to help her cook dinner while our sisters were off doing other things.

To this day, Buddy and I are very good cooks according to our standards. Now when Daymond and Alice grew past the stage of drinking milk and eating baby food, I was prepared to cook a meal for us to eat.

In 2019, the end result of my decision to be a different kind of a father when I was eight was so effectual that it changed the direction of the generation that came after my brother and me.

My oldest son Caleb is a great father to my grandson, Caylem. My daughter Angel is a great mother to my other grandson, Carter and my daughter's husband Devon is a great father as well.

Daymond, my oldest nephew learned from my brother and me how to be a father to his children. Daymond will move heaven and hell to be a part of his children's lives. I have seen him move from one state to another state so that he could have a major role in his son and daughter's lives. And JJ, Daymond's brother, is a great father to his 6 children as well.

From a distance, through the years, as he was growing up, he watched and took note of how involved my brother and I were in our children's lives. We were role models to every male that came after us as to how to be a father.

Over the years I have learned that the thing that causes you the most misery in life is the very thing that wants to get your attention so that you can be used to change it. You just have to decide to be the change agent.

In closing this chapter, I leave you with "Our Deepest Fear" by Marianne Williamson.

> *"Our deepest fear is not that we are inadequate. Our deepest fear is that we are powerful beyond measure. It is our light, not our darkness that most frightens us.*
>
> *We ask ourselves, 'Who am I to be brilliant, gorgeous, talented, fabulous?' Actually, who are you not to be?*
>
> *You are a child of God. Your playing small does not serve the world. There is nothing enlightened about shrinking so that other people won't feel insecure around you.*
>
> *We are all meant to shine, as children do. We were born to make manifest the glory of God that is within us. It's not just in some of us; it's in everyone. And as we let our own light shine, we unconsciously give other people permission to do the same. As we are liberated from our own fear, our presence automatically liberates others."*

CHAPTER 6

BATTLING FOR EVERYTHING REQUIRES THAT YOU IDENTIFY YOUR GOLIATH.

"A champion named Goliath, who was from Gath, came out of the Philistine camp. His height was six cubits and a span. ⁵He had a bronze helmet on his head and wore a coat of scale armor of bronze weighing five thousand shekels, ⁶ on his legs he wore bronze greaves, and a bronze javelin was slung on his back. ⁷His spear shaft was like a weaver's rod, and its iron point weighed six hundred shekels. His shield bearer went ahead of him." (1 Sa 17:4-7)

"Avoiding danger is no safer in the long run than outright exposure. The fearful are caught as often as the bold."- Helen Keller

Earlier in this book, I wrote about my brother persuading me to stand my ground and defend myself against two of my classmates that in some form or another would beat me up every school day of the week.

They did this because I would not fight back. To them, I was easy prey. However, once I was convinced that I had to stand up and fight, which I eventually did, the daily beatings stopped because *I stood up* and put a stop to them.

> The first thing I had to do was **confront** the fear in my head about my two classmates.
>
> The second thing I had to do was **decide** if I wanted to receive 3 beatings or no beatings on that particular day.
>
> And the third thing I had to do was actually **fight**.

My brother helped me realize a valuable lesson at an early age because it taught me to stand up against all *Goliaths* that come to intimidate with size and boldness.

The second Goliath that made his presence in my life was at the early age of 9 from our neighborhood bully nicknamed ES.

One afternoon, I just happened to be in the wrong seat while the older teenage boys were playing dominos in my family's back yard.

ES was losing the game and he assumed that I was cheating and helping another player by telling the other player what he had in his hand.

I was wrongfully blamed for ES losing the game. He flew into an uncontrollable rage and picked-up a sizable stick and hit me in the center of my back as hard as he could leaving a bruise for evidence.

At age 18, ES had a history of terrorizing all children much younger and smaller than himself.

However, he never would bully folks in his age group. My brother and his friends consoled me until I stopped crying. We came up with a plan to seek revenge. We did not seek the counsel of our parents or ES' parents as to how we should proceed. As a matter of fact, no one knew what we were planning but we were determined to stop ES by any means necessary.

The plan to get our revenge and teach ES a lesson that he would never forget was finalized and implemented. Buddy, Darrell, Delvin, and I decided that we were going to stone ES for hitting me in the back with a stick and for terrorizing the neighborhood children.

We found large bricks and put them in four strategic locations that would inflict the most damage on our target. We did not concern ourselves with the consequences of our action because we were driven by anger and revenge.

We wanted ES to stop bullying us. After placing the bricks in the designated areas, we lured ES into the trap. For years we studied his demeanor and behavior; therefore, we knew what would drive him to anger to chase us... and it worked!

We had him just where we planned for him to be and then we let him have every brick we stored for him. We did not stop stoning him until all the bricks were gone from every strategic location.

The plan was executed with perfection. We delivered the stones and the message that went along with it. The message was:

> ES! LEAVE US ALONE!! HE RECEIVED AND ACCEPTED THE MESSAGE BECAUSE ES NO LONGER TERRORIZED US AGAIN.

In 1990, I was 23 years old when I would have to face another Goliath that came in the form of fear and doubt in the area of education. As long as I was just talking about going back to school this Goliath never presented itself to me because I was just talking about returning to college.

Before I get to my story, let me start by explaining, I started my college career at LSU in 1985 immediately after high school. Needless to say, like many other 18-year-olds, I did not do well in my early years of college.

As a matter of fact, in two and half years of attending LSU, I completed just 27-hours. After the fall semester in 1987, I decided that I would not go back to college until I figured out where my purpose and passion was in life. In 1988, I found them both in the

45

area of ministry. After finding my purpose and passion for life, I made plans to get the necessary training.

The plans were made and implemented in 1989, the year Andrea and I got married. I had applied and was accepted as a student at Harding University in Searcy, Arkansas. The plan was for us to remain in Baton Rouge, Louisiana until August of 1990.

My ministry training would start that month. My return date to college was set, now I only had to find money to help pay for it. It was at this moment when Goliath showed up to intimidate me with *fear and doubt*.

My mind was constantly bombarded with who would give me money to go to an expensive private school, plus I had flunked out of LSU, not once but *twice*.

I acknowledge the validity of the premise, but I refused to apply the premise to me because for the first time in my life, I had purpose for my life and my passion to fulfill this purpose was an unwavering hot flame in me. So, I pushed forward to find some financial support.

In May of 1990, for a weekend we would travel to Homewood Church of Christ to visit some friends we had made during the time we had worked as interns, we also used this time to try and seek support from this congregation.

After the Sunday morning worship, we had a brief meeting with Wayne Kilpatrick, the senior minister. We explained to him what we were seeking. In return he informed us that the congregation would not support us because the church's policy was to only help families that were already doing ministry.

However, he told us to give him our proposal and that he would share it with the elders at their next meeting. We thanked him for meeting with us and we left with mixed feelings. Here it was in May and we had not raised the necessary funds. To be honest, I was a little scared, but I stuck with my belief that God was going to come through for us. I did not waver in this belief.

The following Saturday I would receive a phone call from Pat Bell, one of the elders from the Homewood Church of Christ. The phone conversation was the following, "Hello this is Pat Bell from the Homewood Church of Christ, may I speak with Greg?"

I responded, "This is he." Half listening, thinking it may be a phone solicitor.

He cleared his throat, "Wayne shared your ministry proposal with the elders on Monday." Now he had my full attention, "Oh, okay."

"I know Wayne told you the church policy," he started.

"Yes sir, he did." I began bracing myself for failure.

"Well, I like what you and your wife are attempting to do. So, I took your proposal to my wife."

I could feel hope building up inside me, "Really?" He continued, "You see, my wife and I graduated from Harding University and we are University board members."

I was holding my breath and started silently praying to God as he kept explaining, "We both believe in your program so much we are going to support you with twelve-thousand dollars to get you started."

All I could say was "thank you" over and over again. I wanted to explain that through him, God was confirming that me and my family were on the right track. I wanted him to know God had been preparing me for this all of my life.

47

Instead, I just kept saying, "Thank you." Then the shock started to wear off, "I will pay you back as soon as I am able," I promised.

His response to me was "No, the only thing I ask is that when you are able, return the favor to someone else."

My Goliath was silent because Pat Bell and his wife stepped up and said with their action that they believed in my dream of preparing for working in the ministry. Although my Goliath had lost this battle, he still was there to fight against me with doubt.

In August of 1990, Andrea and I made the transitional move to Searcy, Arkansas from Baton Rouge, Louisiana, so that we could start our ministry intense training program at Harding University. It was designed to complete 120 hours of Bible classes along with other courses in a two-year period. Right from the onset this was very intimidating especially from the viewpoint that I had only managed to complete 27 hours of college classes from my first go around of college which was a two-year time span. In the beginning, my biggest fight was with myself.

On a daily basis, I had to encourage myself to stay the course because my mind was full of doubt and fear. I kept my purpose for being in school at the forefront of my mind. I branded this purpose in my mind to keep me motivated.

The next thing I did was to concentrate on taking notes from all of my lectures that suited me and only me. In all of my classes, I would only write down the main points of the professor lectures and just a few points that supported the main points. My notes were arranged in such a way that made sense to me and me only. I did not share my written lecture notes because they were confusing to others.

After my classes, I would study for about four hours daily. Because I studied on a daily basis, I discovered that my test preparation was more of a review session rather than a cram session. Also, during testing time, I would go into the classroom when the professor went into the class to distribute the test material.

My reason for doing this was to protect myself against the doubt and nervousness of other students. I did not want to deal with their issues, I had my own issues. The things I did on a consistent basis paid off because I completed the first term with three B's" and one A giving me a 3.25 GPA. I was very proud of myself for this accomplishment.

The monkey was off my back and I proved I could do well in college. When I look back, this obstacle was no different than the other obstacle I had to overcome in my life. This obstacle was there to make me stronger, just like the other ones that had made me stronger.

The first term was no fluke or accident because I finished my first year of the program with a 3.5 GPA. The Goliath that showed up to discourage me from pursuing my educational training for ministry fought me at every turn, but I stood my ground and fought back because my purpose and passion were worth it.

Over the years, all types of Goliath's have presented themselves in my life. Many of these Goliaths have been nontangible giants. These giants cannot be seen with the physical eye; however, you can see the effects they create in your life.

The nontangible Goliaths come in the form of depression, anxiety, anger, bitterness, mental illness, broken heart, etc.

Nevertheless, whether the Goliath is tangible or nontangible, it shows up to terrorize and intimidate. And it will continue to do so until you put a stop to it. Your Goliath will make you bow down and submit to its will if you don't fight and stand your ground against it.

YOUR GOLIATH IS WILLING TO MAKE YOU A PRISONER WHERE THERE IS NO PRISON. IT WILL DETERMINE WHAT YOU CAN OR CANNOT DO IN LIFE. IT WILL PUSH YOU AROUND UNTIL YOU STOP IT.

In order for you to stop your Goliath from controlling your life, you must be able to identify it. And just how do you do that?

Firstly, you must decide to spend time with yourself for thinking and **reflection**.

It is imperative that you get away from the noise and distractions to unclutter your mind. *Most of your battle is in your mind.* Your mind is your best resource. Your mind is your equalizer. Your mind is your greatest asset. However, your mind can aid your Goliath to fight against you if you don't learn how to use it to your benefit. "Your mind can be your greatest friend if you control it, but if it controls you it can be your greatest enemy." *Notes from Noni*

Secondly, once you start to free your mind of clutter, you can begin to **focus** your mind on your Goliath that wants to destroy you. What is on your mind all the time? It goes to bed with you. It wakes up with you throughout the night and gets up with in the morning.

It goes to work with you. It spends more time with you than your family. It makes you fearful. It depresses you. It makes you angry. It limits your laughter. It is intimidating. And it asks you what are you going to do about it? **Once you recognize that dreadful, frightful, and fearful thing you have just identified your Goliath.**

Now that you know who your Goliath is, you are now ready to do **battle**. It's one thing to identify your Goliath, but it's another thing to fight against it. If you are to utterly defeat your Goliath, you must be fully resolved to do so because the fight will not be finished until one of you is still standing. Howbeit, when you fight you must do it strategically to assure yourself victorious.

CHAPTER 7

BATTLING FOR EVERYTHING REQUIRES THAT YOU FIGHT WITH YOUR OWN TOOLS.

"'I cannot go in these,' he said to Saul, 'because I am not used to them.' So, he took his staff in his hand, chose five smooth stones from the stream, put them in the pouch of his shepherd's bag and, with his sling in his hand, approached the Philistine." (1 Sa 17:39b)

"Embrace your talent and pursue it. You won't believe what you can accomplish."- Anonymous

I closed the last chapter with words of admonitions about fighting your Goliath strategically to assure yourself a victory against your giant.

Fighting strategically requires that you do an **inventory on yourself** to see what type of talents and skills you currently have in your arsenal to fight this crucial battle. If you want to take control of your life, you must fight the fight using the gifts and talents God have designed for you to use.

Over the years, I have met two types of people, generally speaking. You have people that are comfortable in their own skin. And then you have people who are not comfortable in their own skin.

The first group of people spend their time doing things that will develop them into the people they have envisioned for themselves. They focus on things that will help them grow as a person. They understand that they are talented, but they also know that they must do more to develop that talent.

They are willing to work for less money in a job for the simple reason that it serves a higher purpose. They understand that the job is there to help develop them into a better person.

These people are *intentional* in their approach to life.

> They *intend* to be better people. They *intend* to do more as a person. And they *intend* to have more than what they have.

And by instinct, it seems they know how to make the best decision for their lives. These people deal with themselves from an internal perspective.

They know that their greatest assets are always found within them and never outside of them.

These people are not afraid to fight because they know that nothing worth having comes easy or cheap. They are not afraid to fail because they use their failure as teaching lessons to learn from as they move forward.

They are always trying and doing different things because they know that developing new skills will enhance them and add more tools to their arsenal.

> THESE PEOPLE ARE GOLIATH KILLERS.

Now the people who are not comfortable in their own skin are not Goliath killers because they have not developed the necessary skills to do so.

These people deal with life from an external perspective. To them, the external approach of life is greater than the internal approach.

Whenever there is an issue to be resolved in their lives, outside resources are sought first before they look to themselves to solve the problem. Their greatest assets are found in other people rather than from inside of them. They do not trust their own judgement about their own life. The opinion of others carry more weight to them than their opinion on any subject.

Because of their approach to life from an external viewpoint it is impossible for them to fight effectively against their Goliath. This personal giant will continue to control them until a change is made by them. It is imperative that these people change from an external perspective of life to an internal perspective of life if they are to fight effectively against their Goliath.

Change is not easy, but it must happen if you are to be successful. In order to change perspectives, you must learn about yourself and the only way you can learn who you are is to spend time with yourself just like you spend time with others.

You must be **intentional** about reflection during your time alone. You must make time for yourself just as you make time for others. You must decide what is most important to *you*. For me, some time ago, I decided that I would deal with myself from an internal perspective when I sought to redefine myself after I lost my 1st wife and my ministry.

In 2005, just six short years after returning to United States from Venezuela I had become someone that I did not know or like. At this point in life my Goliath was *depression* the result of a failed marriage and ministry. I was just surviving not living.

I hated my position in life with a passion. It was time to transition back into the person that I knew and liked. However, when I was ready for change in my life, I just did not know **how** to make the change. I began to search for ways to improve my life.

For many years, while living in New Orleans, I worked several jobs with no clear direction, I was working just to make money.

Nothing could light my passion like working in the ministry. I wanted to make a difference in my life as well as in the lives of others, but I did not know how to do it outside of working as a servant of God. Nevertheless, I would search until I found something that I could do with *passion and purpose*.

After several years of searching, the thing that I discovered was business. However, learning business was also the catalyst that put me on the journey to deal with myself from an internal perspective.

While living in Alexandria, I started a business called Passion for Life. The focus of this business was to help people improve the quality of their lives by helping them to change from the inside out.

It also was a business where I taught people how to speak Spanish as a second language. Although I was not able to get my business off the ground like I wanted, I was content with the fact that I was able to work my business with vigor and tenacity. These were feelings I had lost for several years because of my pain.

I had begun the process of healing myself from my pain by dealing with me from an internal prospective and sharing my journey with others. Once again, the Goliath that presented itself in my life, this time, in the form of depression found itself on the losing end because I learned how to use my God given abilities to defeat it.

As I reflect back on those rough days when I was at the lowest point in my life, I think that the song "I did it my way" by Frank Sinatra is an ideal way to close this chapter.

It is my prayer that you learn how to solve your problems in life through your internal perspective so that you may find your God given abilities that you may use to defeat your Goliath every time it presents itself in your life.

Now I leave you with the words of "I did it my way."

> "And now, the end is near
>
> And so, I face the final curtain
>
> My friend, I'll say it clear
>
> I'll state my case, of which I'm certain
>
> I've lived a life that's full
>
> I've traveled each and every highway
>
> But more, much more than this
>
> I did it my way
>
> Regrets, I've had a few
>
> But then again, too few to mention
>
> I did what I had to do
>
> And saw it through without exemption
>
> I planned each chartered course
>
> Each careful step along the byway
>
> And more, much more than this
>
> I did it my way
>
> Yes, there were times, I'm sure you knew
>
> When I bit off more than I could chew
>
> But through it all, when there was doubt
>
> I ate it up and spit it out
>
> I faced it all and I stood tall
>
> And did it my way
>
> I've loved, I've laughed, and cried

I've had my fill my share of losing

And now, as tears subside

I find it all so amusing

To think I did all that

And may I say - not in a shy way

Oh no, oh no, not me

I did it my way

For what is a man, what has he got

If not himself, then he has naught

To say the thing he truly feels

And not the words of one who kneels

The record shows I took the blows

And did it my way

CHAPTER 8

BATTLING FOR EVERYTHING REQUIRES THAT YOU NAME AND IDENTIFY YOUR PAST SUCCESSES.

"But David said to Saul, 'Your servant has been keeping his father's sheep. When a lion or a bear came and carried off a sheep from the flock, ³⁵I went after it, struck it and rescued the sheep from its mouth. When it turned on me, I seized it by its hair, struck it and killed it. ³⁶Your servant has killed both the lion and the bear; this uncircumcised Philistine will be like one of them, because he has defied the armies of the living God.'" 1Sa 17:34-36

"I have learned that success is to be measured not so much by the position that one has reached in life as by the obstacles which he has had to overcome while trying to succeed." - Booker T. Washington

What is your aim in life?

As a man, what do you want to accomplish in your life?

What is your plan to get you to your desired end?

What does the end result look like?

Have you ever experienced success in your life?

If *yes*, what steps did you take to give you the desired result you were looking to obtain?

Success breeds success. It has the power to lead you from a lower level to a higher level in your life. A successful template on a lower level can be duplicated on an entirely different level.

Once you have developed a successful template to defeat one obstacle in your life, you may use that same developed template to help you overcome other obstacles in your life. In other words, the template is *transferrable and adaptable*.

However, the key to developing a "Success Template" requires that you have an aim or goal you want to achieve in life.

A Success Template **will not** happen by chance... You can't stumble upon it... Being *Lucky* will not bring it to you... Relying on others alone will not give it to you... And you cannot inherit it.

To create a Successful Template, you must work for it.

It will cost you dearly... You will have to fight for it, it will cost you tears, it will cost you sleep, it will cost you loneliness, it will cost you relationships, and it will cost you pain and heartache.

It will cost you forever being misunderstood. The price is high, and you will have to pay the full price for your success. Are you willing to pay the price?

In 2015, I left the teaching profession to start a vehicular transportation business to help make my goal of financial independence a reality.

The root of my financial independence goals come from the deep-seated curse of poverty and lack that runs deep in my family. In 2007, my oldest sister died in poverty and in 2014, my mother died in poverty.

In both cases, the surviving family members had to pool our monies together to bury them. What a shame, to live and die in poverty. The Goliath that controlled and devastated my family, for years, came in the form of poverty and lack.

This giant is brutal, unmerciful, uncaring, shows no respect, and demands that you stay in your place—which is a *state of helplessness*.

> I WORKED MY BUSINESS DILIGENTLY AND FAITHFUL FOR THREE YEARS TO FIGHT TO DESTROY THIS MERCILESS TYRANT.

However, in 2018, this tyrant would show me that it was not just going to lie down and allow me to walk away from its clutches. I had to close my business for lack of funds to keep it going.

What a huge blow to my fight and desire to overthrow the tyranny of poverty and lack in my life.

> How do you overcome an opponent that is so **oppressive** and relentless to keep you under control?
>
> How do you overcome an opponent that is **ruthless** and will continue to destroy you by any means necessary?
>
> How do you fight on when the **fight** is nearly beat out of you?
>
> Do you wave the white flag to signify that you **surrender**?

These are questions that demand answers.

After closing my business, I stepped back to regroup, to reorganize and to renew my passion to destroy poverty and lack in my life. Because I took time to reflect and examine my situation, I became even more resolved to fight onward.

I decided that I would rely heavily on my past success, not as trophies to boast about, but as motivational tools. I was successful as a father. I was successful as a college student. I was successful at redefining myself. I was successful as a minister. I was successful as a teacher. I was successful as an employee. I was successful at getting back up at every knock down.

I continue to fight to rid my life of poverty and lack because of all my past successes. I will break the stronghold of poverty and lack in my life just as I did with other Goliaths that presented themselves in my life in the past.

In 1990, I returned to college after flunking out of LSU in 1987. When I started at Harding University, my mind was full of doubt. Nevertheless, my goal or aim of preparing myself for ministry gave me confidence to carry on and study hard. In May of 1995, I graduated from college with a 3.3 grade point average.

My successful completion of college gives me hope, determination, confidence, and assurance that I will be successful of becoming financially independent. This is where I created my first Success Template.

After that, I simply followed the template I created to be successful at completing my college degree. It is just a matter of time before my relentless pursuit of financial independence makes my Goliath submit and bow down to my desire of being so.

It is just a matter of time when poverty and lack will be a thing of the past like the other Goliaths that presented themselves in my life. As I mentioned earlier, success breeds success.

In closing, I want to challenge and encourage you to examine your life's experiences. Allow your mind to focus on the success you have had in your life. Once you have identified those victories then use them to propel you into more victories, to create the life you dream and envision for yourself.

CHAPTER 9

BATTLING FOR EVERYTHING ALLOWS YOU TO CHANGE THE DIRECTION OF YOUR FAMILY.

"David said to Saul, 'Let no one lose heart on account of this Philistine; your servant will go and fight him.' [25b] 'The King will give great wealth to the man who kills him. He will also give him his daughter in marriage and will exempt his family from taxes in Israel.'" (1 SA 17:32 & 25b)

"Instead of so much negativity let's shine light on some positive... thanks Dad for being there for Caleb and me. You have instilled principles in us that will be passed on for generations to come, you showed me how a woman should be treated by a man and you taught Caleb how to be a man and now that he has a son I see you through Caleb, I love you Dad." - Angel Phillips Thomas (My daughter)

I have learned that when you decide to be a difference maker and then succeed at being one, your intentional actions affect everything that has some type of connection to you.

When my children were younger, I had the idea that I wanted them to be better than me. I wanted them to be more. I wanted them to do more. And I wanted them to have more. Therefore, I needed to impregnate them with principles that would bring my dream for them to reality at some point in their lives.

So, I planted the seed in them at a very young age. I did things that would challenge their thinking. In elementary school, I used their homework as a tool. Not one time did I ever sit down at the table with them to do homework. I would go over the instructions with them and then checked to see if they understood them.

Once the preliminary things were completed, I left them to struggle with finishing the assignment. If they could not solve a homework problem, I phrased the problem in a different manner and if this did not help, I would put a question mark by the particular problem with a note to teacher for further explanation and clarification. I never gave them the answer to the problem because that was the easy way out. I wanted them to learn that anything worth having required a struggle.

Another thing I did with my children was to take them on field trips to the Housing Projects in New Orleans, Louisiana. This was before hurricane Katrina. We walked around the Magnolia Projects, the Fisher Projects, and the Desire Project.

These projects were some scary and dangerous places to live and here we were walking around them to observe poverty and lack. My purpose for doing this was to teach my children about the power of making choices.

I let them know we were not there to be judgmental. Once we walked through the projects, I only asked them to explain what they saw. Then I finished with explaining to them how important it was to know how to make good decisions and identify bad decisions.

I explained to them that we all have the ability to choose and the choices we make will either benefit us or make us suffer. I impressed upon them that knowing how to *think* was crucial in the ability to distinguish between making good and bad decisions.

My mode of teaching my children was to ask them questions about any given issue. I was more concerned about *how* they thought as opposed to *what* they thought. I would tell them on many occasions that I did not want them giving me answers to question in a way that was to please me, but that I wanted them to give me answers that they thought about and struggled with internally.

I told them that I would support their well thought-through answers whether I agreed or disagreed with them.

My children knew I was not trying to live my life through them because I told them this many times. I knew that I was not going to be around forever, so it was my responsibility to teach and train them how to live independently from me in this life.

> I TAUGHT THEM THAT LIFE WAS HARD AND UNFORGIVING, ESPECIALLY FOR THOSE WHO DID NOT KNOW HOW TO THINK.

My children saw the good, the bad, and the ugly in my life. They saw me struggling with life. I did not hide it from them, but my children also saw me thinking how I was going to get out of my miserable situations. I was living through what I was instilling in them.

It was during these times that I challenged them to read. We would spend many hours at the bookstore reading books and thinking about a better future.

I would plant the idea of being a millionaire by the time they turned 30 in their minds. We would talk about being more, doing more, and having more.

Around this time Caleb was in sixth grade and learned about entrepreneurship. He started a little business of selling rice crispy snacks at the school he was attending. That year, he made a thousand dollars and I was proud to stand back and see how wisely he used his money. He learned about the value of money that he still holds on to this day.

Because I was intentional in the lessons. I was teaching my children when they were younger, it has paid off in ways that blow my mind. Today, Caleb is 27 and Angel is 25 with families of their own.

I wrote earlier that Caleb is a Captain on a tugboat. He put himself through Wheelman School while he was working as a deckhand. He learned what he needed to do by asking questions and reading about what he needed to do. He is a Captain today because he paid the price to become one. Caleb was intentional in his approach being a Captain.

Angel works with a company in Houston, Texas that hired her full-time from Lofton Security. She was the site supervisor for Lofton Security and did such a great job, the company approached her with a job opportunity in 2019. Angel was intentional at being the best supervisor she could be with Lofton Security and it led her to a better opportunity.

She also has an online business called Radiant Love. She does a *Love Talk* Instagram Live weekly talk show with the purpose to uplift, encourage, inspire, and relate. Angel is successful in life because she intends to be successful.

Now, how intentional are you in your desire to change the direction of your family?

How focused are you?

Are you consistent in your action to effect change?

How persistent are you to effect the change you desire?

Are you clear in your mind about the change you want to effect in your family?

I agree whole heartedly with Socrates when he said, "The secret of change is to focus all of your energy, not on fighting the old, but on building the new."

CHAPTER 10

WHAT'S STOPPING YOU FROM BATTLING FOR EVERYTHING AND PLANNING TO WIN? NOTHING WILL CHANGE UNTIL YOU DO!!!

"On hearing the Philistine's words, Saul and all the Israelites were dismayed and terrified. [24]Whenever the Israelites saw the man, they all fled from him in great fear." (1 SA 17:11&24)

Over the years, I have met people who want to make a change in their life, but their desire for change weighs less than the misery they are living, so they never start the process to change.

For many of them, the one thing that I have found that holds them from moving forward is **FEAR**.

    They are fearful of failing.

    They are fearful of what people will think of them.

    They are fearful of disappointing family members.

    They are fearful of succeeding.

    They are fearful of change.

People want their situation to change, but they are fearful to do the necessary things to make the change, so they settle with their misery.

However, if you are reading this book then you have not settled with your misery and you are trying to find positive ways to change your life.

I encourage you to keep fighting and searching for your better life. It is not easy, but the fight is worth the fight. To give you some encouragement, I will use the remaining of this chapter to feed your fighting spirit with some helpful quotes.

INSPIRATIONS

"The size of your success is measured by the strength of your desire; the size of your dream; and how you handle disappointment along the way."
-Robert Kiyosaki

"Observe what the average people around you are doing and if you don't want to end up like them, then do the opposite."
-Alykhan Gulamali

"People with goals succeed because they know where they're going."
-Earl Nightingale

"Don't let the fear of the time it will take to accomplish something stand in the way of your doing it. The time will pass anyway; we might just as well put that passing time to the best possible use."
-Earl Nightingale

"All hard work brings a profit, but mere talk leads only to poverty." -Proverbs 14:23

"You are today where your thoughts have brought you; you will be tomorrow where your thoughts take you."
-James Allen

"Good thoughts bear good fruits; bad thoughts bear bad fruits."
-James Allen

"There is no greater agony than bearing an untold story inside you"
-Maya Angelou

"Optimism is the faith that leads to achievement. Nothing can be done without hope and confidence."
-Helen Keller

"Although the world is full of suffering, it is also full of the overcoming of it." -Helen Keller

"You better live everyday like your last because one day you're going to be right."
-Ray Charles

"If you can't figure out your purpose, figure out your passion."
-T. D. Jakes

"To find yourself, think for yourself."
-Socrates

"I cannot teach anybody anything, I can only make them think." -Socrates

"Whether you think you can, or you think you can't—you're right."
-Henry Ford

"All men's miseries derive from not being able to sit in a quiet room alone."
-Blaise Pascal

"Success is the sum of small efforts—repeated day in and day out."
-Robert Collier

"Start where you are. Use what you have. Do what you can."
-Arthur Ashe

DEDICATION

I dedicate this book to Ms. Maude Phillips—my mother. She was a great woman. Everything that was good, decent, honorable, admirable, trustworthy, and dependable in her she did her best to transfer these qualities into each of her 7 children.

The first thing I learned from my mother was the importance of spirituality in my life. Every Sunday my mother took all of her children ,3 boys and 4 girls, to church. No one was exempt from going to church on Sunday morning no matter what you did Saturday night. That was the law in Ms. Maude's house!!

My mother also had a vision for my brother and me. She wanted us to be better men than what our fathers were, and the men were in the neighborhood we grew up in. There were many things that we could not do. One of those things was hanging out on the street corner like many of the men did.

My mother impressed upon us that if she caught us hanging out on the street corner, she was going to make us a permanent fixture on that same corner. It wasn't until I left my mother's home that my understanding was made clear why my mother was so adamant about my brother Buddy and me not hanging out on the street corner.

I would go home to visit my mother on occasion and during my visits I saw the same men still hanging out on the corner. Before my mother passed away in 2014, she was able to see her vision for her sons become a reality. We became the men she wanted us to be.

We became the fathers that she wanted us to be; she was very proud of Buddy and Greg—her sons!! I am the man I am today because of my mother. I am a fighter because my mother was a fighter. In darkness, I will find my way because my mother found her way through her darkness. I will never quit trying to improve me because my mother never stopped trying to be a better person.

One of her sayings was, "When life hands you a lemon make lemonade out of it." I am an independent man because my mother was an independent woman. I work hard at everything I do because my mother worked hard at everything she did. I am a good father to my children because my mother was a good mother to me.

Thanks Ms. Maude, you were the BEST!!!

REFERRALS

If "Battling for Everything and Planning to Win" has benefitted you in a positive way, please refer it to 10 or more of your family and friends.

Email me to set up speaking engagements

Provide a referral list of family and friends so I can send them information about my book

Send me honest feedback and / or testimonials

glpequippingblackmen@gmail.com

Thank you for your support.

ABOUT THE AUTHOR

Greg Phillips was born in Alexandria, Louisiana on April 17, 1967. Out of the six children that his mother had, he was the only one that was born in his grandmother's home. Greg says that his life can be summed up as fighting for what you want out of life and never living under someone else agenda.

Greg graduated from Abilene Christian University in 1995 with a degree in Theology/Missiology where he began his Success Template

1992 to 1994 he served as a youth minister while attending ACU.

1995 to 1996 he lived in Costa Rica for one year to learn the Spanish language.

1996 to 1998 he served as a missionary in Venezuela.

1999 to 2000 he served as an urban minister in New Orleans, Louisiana.

2000 to 2018 he lived in a place he calls his "personal wilderness." Greg says that many of the Goliaths he faced were doing this time. He describes this time of his life as being in darkness with dim lights. He walked away from God because he perceived that God had walked away from him during some troubling times in his life.

March of 2010 Greg was blessed by reconnecting with a high school classmate, Angela Coleman.

June 1, 2018 Greg had an encounter with God that changed his life and put him back on the path of being God's servant. Greg is forever grateful to God for showing him mercy when he did not deserve it. After many years of being out of ministry God has called Greg back into ministry to minister to the black community with the focus of helping and challenging black men to reclaim their God given authority of leadership which the black community desperately needs. This book is part of Greg's ministry.

June 20, 2015 Angela and Greg married in Baton Rouge, Louisiana where they currently live. Greg says that Angela was the rose he found while climbing up the rough side of the mountain in his life.

Greg is the father of Caleb Phillips (27), Angel Phillips Thomas (25), and London Gibson (17). He is the grandfather of Caylem Phillips and Carter Thomas. Greg and Angela have also become the legal guardians of Najee Jones—Angela's great nephew.

Made in the USA
Middletown, DE
12 March 2024